# Welcome to My Class!

## Count to Tell the Number of Objects

Noah Haeick

INFOMAX
COMMON CORE MATH
READERS

Rosen
Classroom™

New York

Published in 2014 by The Rosen Publishing Group, Inc.
29 East 21st Street, New York, NY 10010

Book Design: Mickey Harmon

Photo Credits: Cover .shock/Shutterstock.com; p. 5 Szasz-Fabian Ilka Erika/Shutterstock.com.

ISBN: 978-1-4777-1919-0
6-pack ISBN: 978-1-4777-1920-6

Manufactured in the United States of America

CPSIA Compliance Information: Batch #CS13RC: For further information contact Rosen Publishing, New York, New York at 1-800-237-9932.

Word Count: 24

# Contents

This is my class.

I see 4 desks.

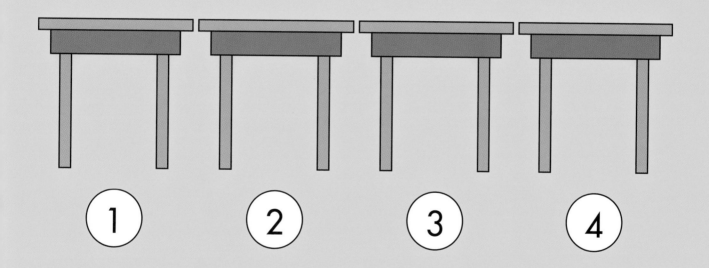

I see 8 pencils.

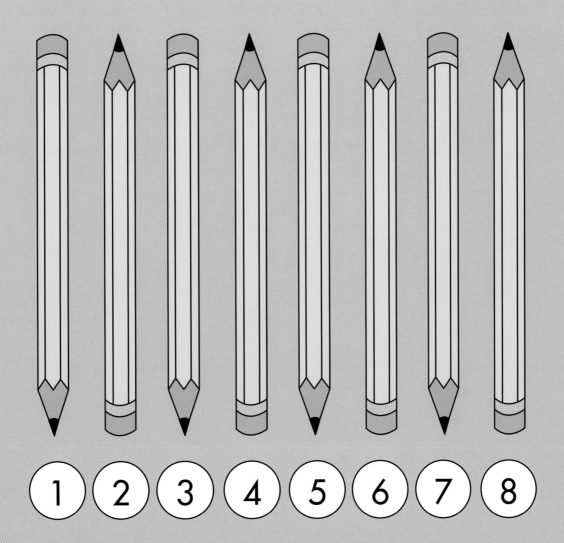

I see 12 crayons.

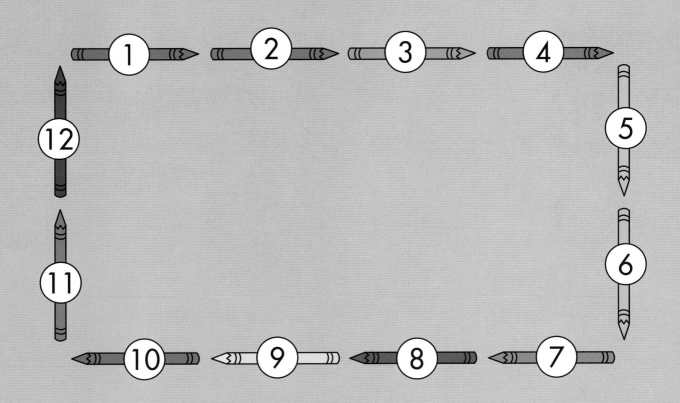

I see 16 books.

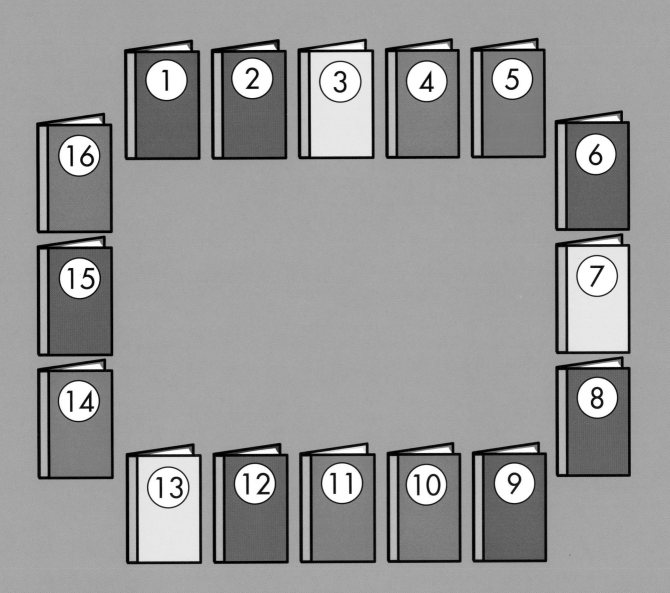

I see 20 toys.

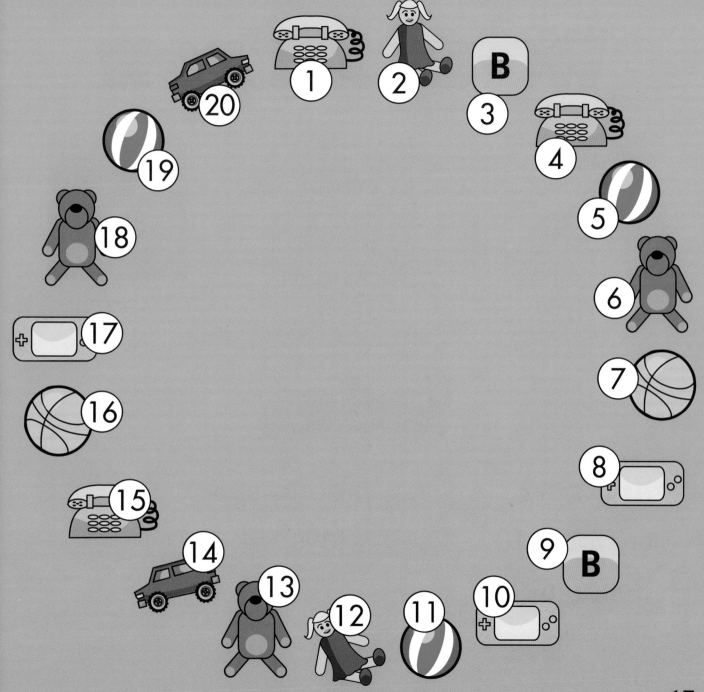

# Words to Know

crayon

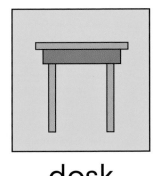
desk

pencil

# Index